WE WILL NOT BE ERASED

The Courage to Rise Above Hate

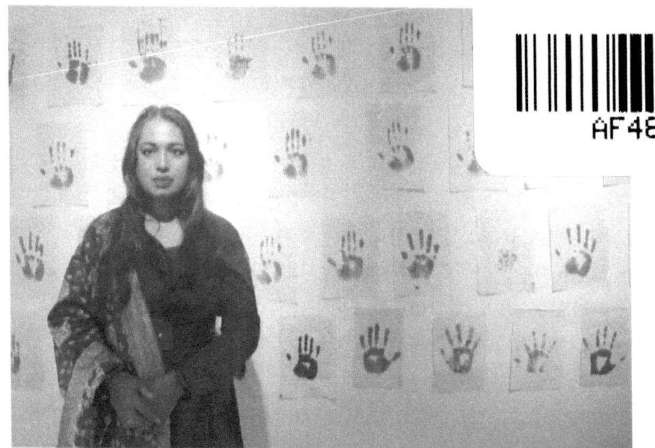

KALKI SUBRAMANIAM

Cover Photo: Alexander Klebe

Cover Art: Kalki Subramaniam

Website: www.kalkisubramaniam.com

notionpress.com

INDIA · SINGAPORE · MALAYSIA

I am one of those thousands
and thousands of transgender
persons who have been
battered, hurt, discriminated
and ignored. But I am not
silenced. Through my activism,
voice,
art and poetry, I stand tall,
I stand for people like me.
We will not be silenced.

This book is a collection of my writings from my diaries, note books and paper collections. It consists of poems, very short stories, notes, monologues, essays, and illustrations. Some of the poems are translations from my Tamil book 'Oru Thirunangaiyin Dairy Kurippu' (ஒரு திருநங்கையின் டைரிக் குறிப்பு).

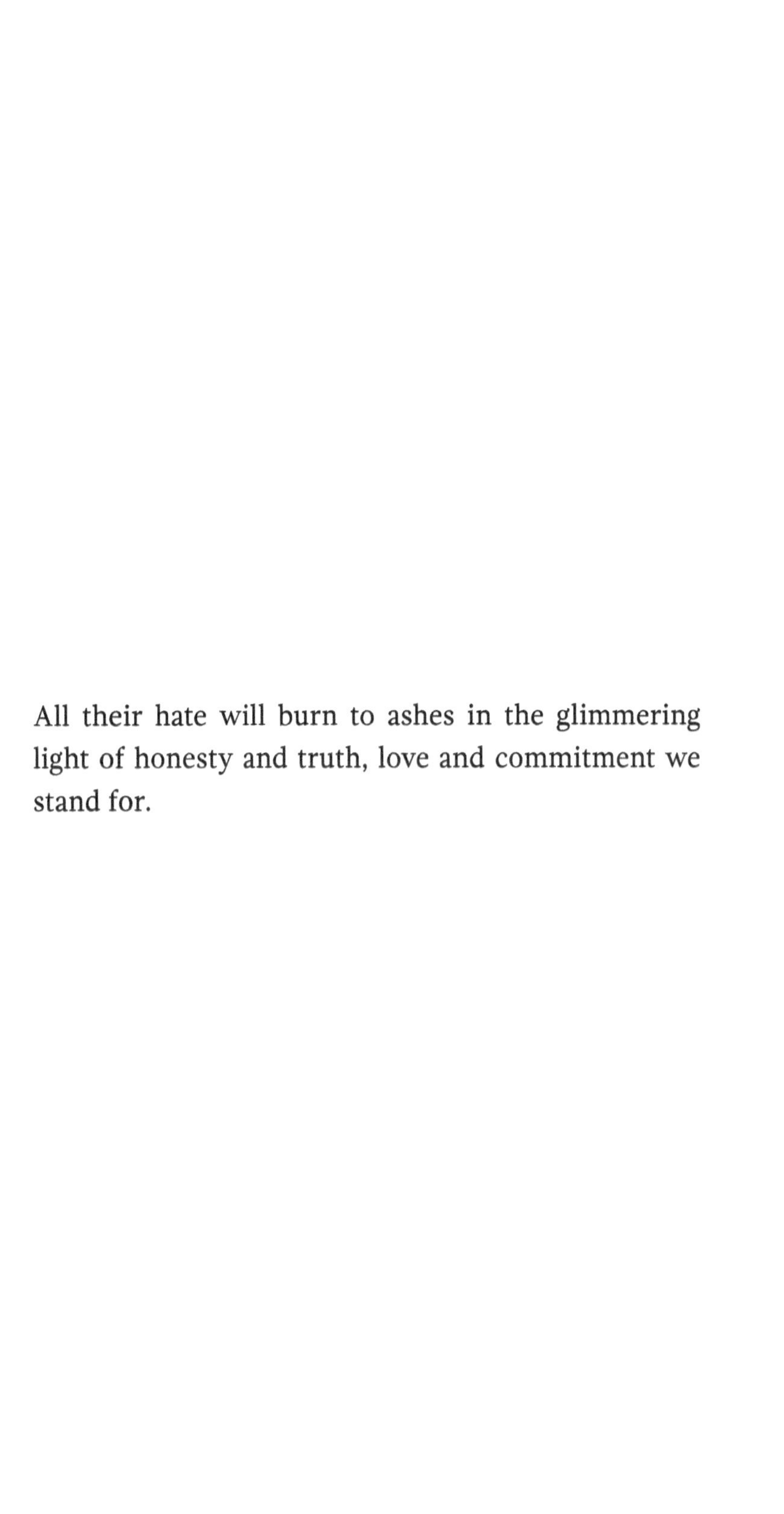

All their hate will burn to ashes in the glimmering light of honesty and truth, love and commitment we stand for.

Contents

Poems

Contents

Very Short Stories

Quotes

Musings

Essays

Contents

About the Author

Kalki Subramaniam is a globally recognized Indian transgender activist, artist, writer, entrepreneur and a renowned international speaker on gender and climate issues. A member of the National Council for Trans Persons, Kalki is the founder of the Sahodari Foundation, an organization dedicated to the social and economic empowerment of transgender people in India.

Kalki has made significant contributions to transgender inclusion in India, sensitizing over a million students nationwide on transgender rights and issues. Her relentless activism champions social justice and equality for transgender people globally. She was a key advocate behind the recognition of legal rights for transgender people by the Supreme Court of India in 2014, a landmark victory for the community.

Through the Sahodari Foundation, Kalki provides free workshops for transgender individuals, promotes their artwork, and supports their livelihoods. Over 500 people have benefited from these workshops, empowering many transgender artists and transforming their lives.

For over a decade, Kalki has been transforming the corporate world with her expertise in Diversity, Equity, Inclusion, and Belonging (DEIB) within the LGBTQIA+ community. As a DEIB speaker and global transgender rights champion, she has addressed in a number of fortune 500 global corporations.

Kalki has received numerous awards for her social work, film performances, and literary contributions. In 2015, Facebook recognized her as one of 12 inspiring women worldwide using the platform for community development and empowerment. In 2016, L'Oreal Paris India nominated her as a 'Woman of Worth' in the arts category.

Her Tamil poetry collection, 'Kuri Aruthean' (குறி அறுத்தேன்), was published in 2014. Kalki made history as the first transgender actor in India to play a lead role in a major motion picture, 'Narthaki'.

Kalki has mentored hundreds of transgender individuals, many of whom have become role models for other young transgender people, working as doctors, artists, entrepreneurs, teachers, and corporate managers. As an artist and entrepreneur, Kalki has exhibited her work in India, Europe, and the USA.

Her international recognition includes a standing ovation at Harvard University's India Conference in 2017, an invitation to present her poetry, art, and activism at the Schwules Museum in Berlin in 2018, and her appointment as the International Ambassador for Life of TransAmsterdam in the Netherlands in 2019.

In 2021, Kalki released her first English book, 'We Are Not The Others,' a collection of poems, essays, art, and monologues. The book is now included in the Harvard Business School Library. In 2022, paintings by Kalki and five of her transgender students were showcased at the University of South Florida, a significant honour for the Indian queer community. That year, she also received the prestigious Radhika Sen Memorial Award from Plan India for the Red Wall Project.

In October 2022, Kalki returned to Harvard and also spoke at Yale, Cornell, Rutgers, and the University of Pennsylvania on activism, art, and literature. In August 2023, she launched her designer artistic wear, Kals Apparel, at Bangalore Fashion Week. In November 2023, she was invited to speak at California State University Northridge and Google Venice. In December 2023, the Indian government appointed her as the Southern Region Representative of the National Council for Trans Persons (NCTP).

In January 2024, Kalki released her third book (in Tamil), 'Oru Thirunangaiyin Diary Kurippu' (ஒரு திருநங்கையின் டைரிக் குறிப்பு). In April 2024, she was invited to speak at the University of British Columbia in

Vancouver, Canada, on Sexual Orientation and Gender Inclusion as part of their Dean's Distinguished Lecture series. In November 2024, Kalki was conferred the title 'Gender Justice Queen' by the Deputy Mayor of Amsterdam Touria Meliani in Netherlands at the 10th anniversary of the TransAmsterdam organization.

On March 2025, The Hindu group presented Kalki with the 'Diversity, Equality and Inclusion Champion' Award, for her tireless work in educating and sensitizing society and fostering diversity, equity and inclusion across India in diverse fields.

Kalki's works of literature in English and Tamil have been added to the educational curriculum in a number of colleges and universities in India. She continues her tireless work advocating for the rights of the LGBTQI+ community and promoting transgender inclusion at all levels of society.

Foreword

We Will Not Be Erased' is Kalki's fourth book and second book in English. As in her first volume, 'We Are Not The Others', she not only shares her reflections and her social criticism, but also her personal strength and resilience. She succeeds in expressing the complexity of the life situations of trans people in India. With great openness, she talks about her own feelings and her resulting mission to strengthen the trans community mentally, gain social recognition for them and improve their living conditions.

A gifted poet, author and painter, transgender activist Kalki Subramaniam uses different literary genres to elegantly express her thoughts. Poems, short stories, diary entries and essays express her anger at social conditions, but also her vulnerability, self-confidence and unbridled will to fight for change, justice, human rights, social participation and acceptance in families. She critically questions norms and conventions and calls for alternative ways of thinking: What constitutes a family? What is femininity?

In the chapter Musings, she contrasts her early diary entries from 2007 with more recent entries from

2023 and 2025, allowing us to participate in her own development process. One of several insights can be found in The Soul: 'The real me has no gender, all of us have no gender'. Her poem The War is illuminating, dealing with displacement, homelessness, loss of family, pain, fear and violence. As a trans person, she does not have a unique destiny, but sees herself as a compassionate part of a larger community of victims of war, displacement and oppression. However, she does not remain a powerless victim, but develops an immense strength to fight against all this and survive.

It is emotionally touching when she writes about her longing to be a mother or about her childhood memories, about the loneliness of a child who is bullied as 'the boy who is feminine'. This leads to withdrawal from everything, from friends and family, and culminates in loneliness, writing poems and drawing. Finally, she finds security in a group of trans women. She is very aware that it was the unconditional love and support of her family that made her the strong fighter she is today.

In her essay 'Why I chose to be an activist', she sums up her demand: we don't need sympathy or pity, but respect, equal rights, humanity and compassion.

'We Will Not be Erased' is a remarkable book. It challenges us to rethink trans identity. We must question our cis perspective. Dialogue with gender-diverse people like Kalki Subramaniam opens up new horizons of understanding. Suddenly, the reasons why things are the way they are become clear, and that they don't have to stay that way. It allows us to emerge cautiously optimistic that we can change them, and how.

Dr. Elisabeth Schömbucher
Retired Professor of Anthropology
University of Würzburg, Germany

A Note

Kalki made history as the first transgender actor in India to play a lead role in a film called 'Narthaki'. A gifted polymath, this powerful book of hers is an earthquake. She has combined poetry, essays, stories, and art to document her journey and the struggles of the transgender community. Kalki doesn't ask for pity or charity; she demands rights, dignity, and respect. Her writing is a rallying cry for inclusion in education, employment, and policy-making.

Through her lines:

"Every trans person, rejected by family, made a refugee in their own land, knows the gut-wrenching pain of Palestinians, the Rohingya, the Eelam Tamils... we are all fighting the same damn war," she draws a bold connection between the struggles of the transgender community and global crises like the Palestinian struggle, the Rohingya refugee crisis, and the Eelam Tamil displacement.

She questions stereotypes within the transgender community itself, challenging to redefine what it means to be a woman:

"Femininity isn't just about being quiet and pretty. It's about power, strength, intelligence, and breaking free.

Murugadoss Arunachalam,
Film Director and Producer

Another Note

In a world that often silences the vulnerable, these poems rise as fierce affirmations of survival and hope. Written by Kalki who has known the plights of displacement, grief, and transcendence, this collection offers an intimate and courageous glimpse into the resilience of the human spirit. Through vivid storytelling and heartfelt reflection, she as a trans woman charts her journey through loss, awakening, and self-acceptance. Here, the margins speak—and their voice is unstoppable. Beneath flesh, beyond labels, the human soul seeks its truth. In this collection, Kalki shares her hard-earned realization that identity is more than body, more than gender—it is the indomitable spirit that rises, again and again, from fire and grief.

In this deeply moving collection, Kalki as a trans woman lays bare her soul, weaving together her personal odyssey with the broader wounds of humanity. Her poems are not mere records of pain; they are cries of resistance, meditations on identity, and songs of survival. With a language that is at once simple and piercing, she invites readers into a world where suffering births strength and where every scar becomes a badge of honour.

In "The War," she feels the pain of distant lands—Ukraine, Congo, Myanmar, Gaza, and Eelam—as if it were carved into her own flesh. Through the rhythmic refrain "she feels them all," she dissolves the boundaries between personal and collective suffering. Her own marginalization becomes a mirror to global injustices. Yet even as she mourns, she refuses to be defeated. From brokenness, she rises—a phoenix, a lioness—waging a furious battle for dignity and respect in an unequal world.

"Death" shifts the gaze inward, chronicling an endless procession of loss. Each memory—a touch, a letter, a smile—is tenderly recalled, yet becomes another stone in the monument of grief. Death ceases to be a moment; it becomes a companion, a heavy atmosphere she breathes daily. In sparse, aching lines, the poet captures the numbing sorrow of losing not just loved ones, but pieces of herself.

In "Hear us Tyrant!," grief and anger ignite into a declaration of immortality. Against tyranny, against oppression, the poet asserts the resilience of queer existence. Like the mythical bird, she and her community rise from the ashes of hatred, bearing witness to the truth that cannot be silenced. The poem beats with a defiant heart, affirming that identity is eternal, and justice, inevitable.

"Zero" takes us into a more intimate terrain, recounting the journey from a masculinity that felt like imprisonment to the liberation of living as a trans woman—and the painful social abandonment that followed. Stripped of familial love and societal acceptance, she embraces a radical solitude. To become "Zero" is, paradoxically, an act of self-possession: choosing invisibility over violation, choosing to exist on her own terms.

Finally, "The Soul" lifts the collection into the realm of the spiritual. Beyond bodies, beyond the rigidities of gender, the poet glimpses the ultimate truth: that the soul is without labels. In luminous, meditative verses, she unveils a vision where identity transcends flesh and prejudice. This poem reframes all that came before—struggle, loss, pride—into a timeless revelation: that at our core, we are all one, genderless, infinite, free.

Together, these poems compose a symphony of pain, defiance, and profound insight. The poet's voice, tender yet unyielding, transforms personal vulnerability into a universal call for empathy, justice, and awakening. In a world that so often denies trans women their right to exist, these poems stand—luminous and unbreakable—as proof that no soul can be erased.

Dr Shantichitra K
Professor, Department of English,
SRM institute of Science and Technology

Poems

The War

She sees a picture of a dead child
and she feels them all.

the unbearable pain of the
dying soldiers in Ukraine and in Russia,
the harrowing silence
of the dead children in Congo,
the mounting hunger of
the falling humanity in Myanmar,
she feels them all.

The husbands dug out from
beneath the debris in Gaza
and the weeping wives in Israel,
the silent cry of siblings
lost in the war for Eelam,
the ceaseless sexual assault
on the terrified children in Congo,
she feels them all.

The helpless outcry of the fathers
who lost their sons and daughters
in Yemen,
the tremulous voices of the mothers
whose homes have been bombed
in Kashmir,
she feels them all.

she knows displacement,
she knows homelessness,
she knows losing a family,
she knows the chilling fear,
and the ignominious oppression,
she knows them all.

She begs at traffic signals by day,
beds with strangers by night,
she is a refugee at home,
for being real, for being right.

She claps in fury,
she claps in grief,
against power, against war,
against poverty, against greed.

She was broken into pieces,
but now she rises as phoenix.
she was silenced and striped,
but now she roars like a lioness.

She is a raging warrior,
this is her battle for survival
her battle for dignity and respect -
for herself, for people like her,
for every silenced voice,
against an unequal world,
for a world she dreams,
for a world that gleams.

* * * * *

Death

I remember the death
of my best friend,

I still can see
her vacant lifeless eyes,

I still can hear
of her weeping voice,

I still can read her letters
though words are blurred
by her fallen tears,

I still can recall
her smile braving
the impact of her pain,

I can still feel the
pricking pieces of
her broken heart,

I remember
her last warm hug,
I remember
her slender palm holding mine,

I remember
her last laughter,
I remember
her last journey.

and then
I remember
another friend,

another death,
another loss,

and another,
and still another.

I lost count.

Then death
becomes my life,

my darkened eyes
dry of shedding tears,
and my diminished soul
crippled and lifeless.

Death becomes my existence.
Death becomes Me.

* * * * *

Hear us Tyrant!

Your brutal tyranny
refuses our existence,
your iron fist
strangles our necks,
we will not be erased.

your outright ignorance
strips off our rights,
your stinking prisons
beat us to death,
and your hatred
burns us to ashes,
we will not be erased.

hear us tyrant!
hear us clown!

We will not beg you
for our existence,
we will not seek
pardon from you,

we will not hide,
we are children of pride,
we will not be erased.

Fools come in disguise,
fools sit on the throne,
fools come and go,
we will not be erased.

From time immemorial,
we were in the past,
we are in the present,
we will be in the future,
we are forever!

* * * * *

Zero

Her masculinity was a prison
she thought,
she planned meticulously
and got rid of it.

The sooner she got rid of it,
her family got rid of her.

She had an awakening
that femininity is a Blessing,
a new life, so she thought.

Now,
living openly as a Trans woman,
she understood that
the saree she robed was
for a man to disrobe.

She knew them, their motives,
She knew them, their conspiracies,
She absconded.

-38-

She got rid of the world,
to be no one, None, Zero.

* * * * *

The Dance

Struggling to accumulate
their life energy
and raise their Kundalini,
men and women
inhaled and exhaled
in symphony.

She unloaded her sanctity
and danced on
nothingness.

She ripped herself
and was Reborn.

Her Metamorphosis.

She grew freedom wings,
she bloomed like vibrant springs,
newly born.

Sense and
Sensibility alike,
she became
awake.

She danced
and danced
on her dead life,
celebrating herself,
in an orchestrated
symphony of her own.

She rebirthed.

* * * * *

A Mouth Full of Elixir

My non-existent uterus,
my empty breast,
my unborn child.

I wanted my breasts
brimming with milk,
flowing from my heavens
to be sucked in peace
by a gigging infant.

A baby of my own.

Thoughts sweep me
like waves,
I was never obsessed
for a child,
I just wanted to
to be a mother,
at least for a day.

I blessed mothers
with little children
lying on their shoulders,
or lying on their laps.

Sometimes I smelled
the scent of motherhood
in the lips of the babies,
their cry was my lullaby,
I would be a mother
for a split second.

Closing my eyes in bliss,
I would bless the babies
and move to the next coach.

I never ever
longed to be a mother,
I just wished to be,
at least for a day.

Then one day in a train,
an infant stopped crying
and smiled at me,
one gleeful smile and

I saw God.
I teared up and cried in joy,
with my eyes wide open,
and a heart that turned lotus,
I walked fulfilled.

Life follows me.

* * * * *

The Dress

When I embraced
my authentic self,
my feminine beauty
broke the barricades,
cascading my body.

In the jubilation of
joy and celebration,
in the exuberating
sashay of liberation,
I found myself
to be the
most beautiful
woman in the world.

ah...
the burst of
my orange lipstick,
the jasmine flowers,
the sequin saree,

my flauntingly
feminine graceful walk,
all caught
their attention.

They stared at me,
they admired,
so, I thought.
aiyo..
they mocked
and grinned at me.

"Your dressing
Is abnormal,
gaudy and absurd,
why don't you people
dress normal?
why do you want to show
yourself a transgender?"

They questioned me.

Why shouldn't I
show who I am?

What is your 'normal'?
What makes me absurd?
Who are you
to tell me that?
Who are you
to judge me?

My dangling beads,
my jingling bangles,
my chiming anklets,
my rustling red saree,
and my orange lipstick,
all of this, I bought.

I bought it
with my own money,
not yours.

now, move away!

* * * * *

The Soul

when I first
understood my real Self,
my authentic Identity
and crafted my body,
I still didn't
completely find
who I really am.

I decided only
on how I must be
seen by people,
I thought
this is what is
all about me,
all of me.

Now, do I feel
complete now?

No, not at all.

I now understand that,
this body
is just a tool,
a messenger, a shirt,
that embraces and carries
my throbbing soul.

The truth is,
the ultimate truth is,
my real me
has no gender.

All humans on earth
carry their bodies,
and the gender labels
forced upon us.

The truth is,
all of us
have no gender.

All of us.

At the end,
we all will someday

wake up to the truth

that the chasing

was worthless,

and that

our souls

are Genderless.

* * * * *

If living authentically is
a crime,
Then I'd be serving a
life sentence.

I am the Sculptor: I am the Sculpture

Waking up to
my authentic self,
I denied
my masculinity,
a toxic to me.

I embraced femininity
in penance of
much pain,
what a long long wait!

The man is gone,
the woman has bloomed,
my long hair, my soft skin,
beauty and charm.

I have become myself,
my true Self, I thought.

But why do
women around me,
none of them celebrate
their womanhood?

Why didn't they
like themselves
in the mirror?

"Womanhood is a prison"
they said.

"Doesn't matter
if we are men or women,
let them treat us
first as humans"
they said.

I understood.

I understood now
that my journey
of self-discovery
isn't over,
my search

for self-realization
still continues,
and my search
for self-respect,
truth and freedom
has just began.

I now
seek to connect
with my real purpose.

I travel, I read,
I think, I teach,
I share, I laugh
finding a meaning,
finding a purpose,
finding the truth,
with the Universe.

* * * *

Your People

"Your people
harass me
in trains,
they touch me,
they extort money,
I fear them",
said an elderly gentleman.

Sir, Listen!
let me tell you,
unless you stop
your contempt,
your judgement,
and your hatred on us,
unless you stop
spewing venomous words
and stop describing us
as disgusting,
unless you stop moving
to another seat
when one of us sits near you,

unless you Understand
that we are humans
and we deserve respect,
love and friendship,
unless you understand
we have a stomach
and we are hungry,
unless your eyes
show compassion
at least in a glace,
and unless you stop
calling us 'Your people',
and understand
that we are all
the same people,

your fear will continue.

* * * *

The Story

Some of
our lives
are short stories,

some of us
are novels,

only a few of us
live as poems,
and poetry of
different kinds.

some live as sonnets,
some as ballads,
some as verses,
and some as Haikus.
and some
can't be classified.

I only wish
those of us,

whose lives
are abrupt
short stories
and tiny tales,
could change
it all into
eternal poems.

* * * *

The Rebel

Ay woman,
when will
you rebel
against them,
those who trumpet
your puberty?

when will
you rebel
against marrying
a stranger?

when will
you rebel
to be You?

why should
your belly bulge
in a year,

or else they stab
you with words
so sharp that
your heart
bleeds in pain,

you must live
as a good wife,
serving your husband,
serving your children,
serving your in-laws,
serving.

and yes...
yes yes yes
you must learn to
nod your head,
isn't it?

when will
you rebel
to be You?

what about
your Ambitions,

your Passions,
and your Desires?
Why do you
burn them in the
wedding fire?

You work hard
for them,
and forget
the Fire in You,
and if I ask you why,
you tell me with guilt
"this is what
women have
done forever".

When will
you rebel to be you?

I wish
you were born
like me,

to be free,
to live authentically,

breaking the chain of lies.

We don't
menstruate,

we don't
marry a stranger,

we don't marry.

no one asks
us why
or why not?

No one cares.

We may
live in slums,
and struggle
to meet our ends,
but with us
you will know,
the real meaning
of being you.

We may wander
we may beg,
but with us
you will know,
how to liberate
your soul
and be just You.

With us you will
learn that life is an
exploding lava,
and not
a melting candle.

With us you will
dance, sing,
laugh, cry,
be loud and
be Yourself.

Tell me,

when will
you rebel
to be You?

-65-

when will you be
You?

* * * *

The Mirror

Every day I look
at the mirror,
and I don't see Me,

I see him and
he is not Me.

Can this
mirror mirror me?

this mirror lies
and all mirrors
I see
lie to me.

The real Me
is caged,

is hidden,

is trying to
break Free,

when all mirrors lie
the true mirror
is my Self.

I keep it safe
with a hope that
one day,
my mirror
will see the Light,
the Truth,
the Me.

That is the day,
I will walk free,

As She.

* * * * *

The Tamarind Tree

The tamarind tree
in my village was
the Mother.

In her branches lived
the chicks cuddling
their mothers' feather.

In Sunrise and Sunset,
they called, they chirped,
they cawed; they sang.

They lived with us.
Some alone, Some as pair,
they flocked as family
and lived in harmony.

One fateful morning
a group of men came,
"We won the bid,
we own her now"

they grinned.
Ravaging machines,
they felled the Mother.

She was killed.

With her fell
hundreds of chicks
crumbling in nests,
we screamed and yelled,
we cried and wept,
they cut her in pieces
and took her away.

Roots were in shreds,
scattered and laid,
victim to viciousness.

The Mother was there
before I was born,
the ruthless corruption
consumed her
and she was gone.

The village now a desert
silent and dead,
powerless and paralysed,
we mourn; we sob.

They robbed our peace,
for wood and for greed.
The wind settled dust,
sweeping all dying seed.

They took our mother,
where do we go?
Will life return,
or sorrows grow?

* * * * *

Dreams of Colour

Swimming in dreams
of shimmering hope,
I sway and raise
my brush from colours,

I strike and create
the canvas in delight,
I open a world of light,
my art is from my soul.

What beauty!
what magic!
I paint with joy,
a genderless being,
an epitome of human beauty.

Neither he nor she,
some parts like me,
the painting smiles in Glee.

Oh, the life of being Free
I wish I could just as well be!

* * * * *

The Shop

I walked to the first shop,
stepping in the front,
I clapped louder,
clap, clap..
I begged for alms,
"You are ugly, go away"
he said,
I stumbled.

I walked to the second shop,
stepping in the front,
I clapped louder,
clap, clap..
I begged for alms,
"You are a shame, go away"
she said,
I wept.

I walked to the third shop,
stepping in the front,
I clapped louder,

clap, clap..
I begged for alms,
"Disgusting! never come here"
they said,
I was heartbroken.

I walked to the fourth shop,
stepping in the front,
I clapped louder,
clap, clap..
I begged for alms,
"You are a curse, go away"
he said,
I felt so small.

I walked to the fifth shop,
stepping in the front,
I clapped louder,
clap, clap..
I begged for alms,
"You look like a man, go away"
she said,
I felt ashamed.

I walked to the sixth shop,
stepping in the front,

I clapped louder,
clap, clap..
I begged for alms,
"You people are worthless, go away"
they said,
I was terrified.

I walked to the seventh shop,
stepping in the front,
I clapped louder,
clap, clap..
I begged for alms,
"You people are a nuisance, go away"
he said,
I cried.

I walked to the eighth shop,
stepping in the front,
I clapped louder,
clap, clap..
I begged for alms,
"You prostitute, go away"
she said,
I stammered.

I walked to the ninth shop,
stepping in the front,
I clapped louder,
clap, clap..
I begged for alms,
I don't want to see you, go away"
they said,
I wiped my tears.

they all shamed me,
they all judged me,
they all ignored me,
they all laughed at me.

One day,
One fine day I stopped begging,
I halted, I grounded,
I began to think.

'Rise' said an inner voice,
that is when I decided
I need to break this chain of hate,
I need knowledge,
I need power,

I need strength,
I need to be free.

I avidly studied,
I learned skills,
the darkness faded
and light filled in,
I steadily climbed.

I opened a shop
in the same street,
I sold good food,
people flocked.
all of them who were mean,
they all came cringing,
waiting in my shop
for my food.

I smiled; I forgave them.
I served with love,
light filled in Me.

* * * * *

Very Short Stories

Love is…

"Would you marry me when I become a complete woman?" she asked.

"I would marry you however you are, I see you, your heart, you are complete. I love your imperfections and perfections. You are always a woman to me and I love you" he said.

They kissed.

* * * * *

The Noose

She pulled the noose of the rope in to her head,

Tirrring... Tirrring...

She hesitated for a moment, got down and picked up the phone,

"Hello"

"Hey Sandhiya, your mother asks you to come back home"

Sandhiya smiled in joy.

* * * *

The Mermaid

Once upon a time, A mermaid lived in the Indian Ocean. She was so fascinated by the legs of the fishermen who came to the ocean. She wanted to marry one of them. One evening while she was swimming near the shores, she was caught by a fisherman. He wanted to sell her to a circus and make money. He was mesmerised by her beauty. At an unexpected moment, she bit the fisherman on his legs and escaped. She was no more fascinated by legs and thought 'Humans with legs are mean'. She never ever again wanted to marry a man.

* * * * *

Ravi

Ravi stood up. He touched his chest and felt the emptiness.

He was very happy and felt like an unbearable load has been lifted from his body. That evening, he went to the Shiva temple, sat at a corner and meditated.

"God, how you created me was your gift to me, How I create myself now is my gift to you. Whoever I am, whatever I am becoming, I am still your child. Even when the entire world may reject me, you are my only hope, you are all I have"

Ravi was in deep silence and prayed Ardhnari with fulfilment.

His heart was light like a feather. He walked home with pride feeling as the most perfect man in the world.

* * * * *

DNA

"No matter how much medicines you take, how many surgeries you do, you cannot change your DNA, you are still a man" mocked a man to me.

"Doesn't matter to us, we know us, what about you? No matter how much money you have, how many offices you hold, and how many countries you have travelled, you are still ignorant, narcissistic, insensitive and a big time Moron" I said.

* * * * *

Them and Us

"These ones are always like this", said the lady to the man next to her pointing at me and my friend. A mean judgement about us.

"Those ones are always like that", said my friend pointing them in rage. "Chee!" She spat. We walked away.

* * * * *

Chandana

Chandana's head spun. She froze with shock, confusing and tears swelling up her eyes. Her home, a 10x10 square foot room in an old housing board building in a North Chennai slum, was flooded with rainwater. To her shock, she found a thick blanket of oil spills mixing and clogging with the rainwater inside. It was sticking to and ruining what little she had left. She didn't know where the oil had come from.

Since the devastating tsunami years ago, heavy rains had chased her from place to place. For a transgender woman like her, renting a place was a horrifying challenge. Her only refuge had been places like the Coovum riverside slums, where the monthly rent was affordable.

Her family had chased her out when she came out as a trans person during her 10th-grade year. To survive, she resorted to begging and sex work, while managing to complete a B.A. degree. Because she had studied in a Tamil medium school, she struggled to speak fluent English. However, she was skilled in computers and was searching for a front office job.

It had been terribly difficult to get placed due to her gender identity. Only in the past few years had some large companies begun offering job opportunities for transgender persons. She had attended several interviews with her degree certificate but was rejected because of her gender identity. She didn't give up and was desperately trying to get a job, a life away from sex work and begging. It was her only hope.

Just two days ago, a corporate company had offered her a job. She was overjoyed. Finally, her life held hope and the promise of a dignified future. She was to submit her certificates the day after tomorrow and begin work.

The rains and flood had washed away her home. Water and oil had seeped into her trunk, where her certificates were stored. The papers were stuck together and completely stained with oil and dirt. She tried her best to remove and clean them, but she couldn't.

Chandana burst into a loud cry and fell in the water. She couldn't believe what had happened. What will she do? How can she undo all this? She knew how difficult it would be to obtain replacements for her certificates. It will be an impossibility. The unchecked encroachment on Chennai's water bodies had led to this disaster, a result of greediness and corruption of the rich and powerful. The devastating impact had fallen on thousands of poor people like her, who had lost everything.

In a couple of days, the waters began to recede. She took her ruined rexine handbag and travelled by the metro train to the East Coast Road. She began to beg from shop to shop.

*   *   *   *   *

Let them talk hate,
Let us spread Love.

Quotes

* * * * *

Transgender individuals deserve love, family, and equal rights, just like anyone else, regardless of their ability to conceive.

* * * * *

* * * * *

Climate Change is the newest and biggest threat to the vulnerable transgender communities around the world. Governments should include the transgender community in climate crisis policies. So far, we've been dealing with problems tied to our very existence. I fear climate change will disrupt our lives further if we don't step up now. The vulnerability of transgender individuals during natural disasters calls for inclusive policies that ensure their safety, protection, and empowerment, addressing the unique challenges we face in times of climate change.

Governments must prioritize the safety and empowerment of vulnerable communities, including the transgender community, when creating climate crisis policies. This is crucial as climate change exacerbates existing inequalities and risks.

* * * * *

* * * * *

Four trans women living together? Family. Two trans men building a life? Family. A trans man and woman finding love? Family. A cis man and a trans woman creating their own dynamic? Family. A woman and a trans man defying expectations? Family. A non-binary individual finding their chosen family? Damn right, that's family too. The old definitions were always excluding, designed to oppress. Real families are built on love, respect, and chosen bonds, not some outdated, bigoted ideal.

* * * * *

* * * * *

So many trans folks are forced to beg on the streets, driven to sex work just to survive. And the *only* reason is the pathetic, systemic failure of our schools and colleges to teach *anything* real about gender and sexuality. Ignorant schoolmates, bigoted teachers—they bully and shame countless trans kids out of an education. And that same toxic, prejudiced ignorance, passed down through generations, is what pushes trans people onto the streets, condemns them to begging, forces them into sex work. It's a disgusting, deliberate, shameful cycle of ignorance and oppression, and it needs to be smashed.

* * * * *

* * * * *

Stop "correcting" kids who don't fit your narrow gender boxes. Embrace them. Understand them. Hitting, punishing, shaming—it won't "fix" them. It'll just break them. Raise them to be *brave*. Support their education. Protect them from the bullies and predators in schools. Monitor their lives. Talk to their teachers. Talk to them. If they're safe from that toxic environment, they'll thrive. I beg you: don't let this generation of kids suffer the way I did.

* * * * *

* * * * *

For every trans spirit: Be brave, let kindness bloom, and claim the world that's rightfully yours.

* * * * *

* * * * *

They shunned me for being trans, tried to drag me down to their level. But as they grovelled to pull at my heels, I used their backs as a stepping stone. Let them try their petty attempts to trip others—I'm shoving them aside, clearing a path for my trans family, and we're taking what's rightfully ours.

* * * * *

* * * * *

Every trans person, rejected by family, made a refugee in their own land, knows the gut-wrenching pain of the Palestinians, the Rohingya, the Eelam Tamils, the Syrians, the Ukrainians and all the war victims – we know what it means to be displaced, hunted, and denied basic human rights. We're all fighting the same damn war.

* * * * *

* * * * *

So many trans women, even some of my closest friends, have told me they feel pressured to perform this tired, stereotypical version of "femininity"— flowers in their hair, draped in sarees, all sweetness, shyness, and demure bullshit. They're told by senior transwomen that's what being a woman means. I call it bullshit. Femininity isn't just about being quiet and pretty. It's about power. It's about strength. It's about intelligence. It's about reaching the summit, breaking free, burning with desire, it is about living the life the way you wanted. It's about everything but the restrictive boxes society tries to shove us into.

* * * * *

* * * * *

We don't need your pity, your useless sympathy. Trans people don't need your tears; we need our damn rights recognized. We're tired of being either mocked or "pitied," like we're some fragile, broken things. The pity party is more dangerous than the open hatred. Treat us like equals. Basic human decency—that's the bare minimum. What good does your pity do? Keep it to yourself; we'll take our respect.

* * * * *

* * * * *

What do you know about love? Love in all its glorious, technicolour forms—that's our reality. Trans women may love cis men, cis women, trans women, trans men, non-binary folks, intersex folks, even themselves. Trans men? Same damn thing. Love doesn't discriminate. You, with your narrow, black-and-white view, watching our rainbow lives like some kind of spectacle—you're not different from us. What, you think you're somehow better? Love is a raging river, a playful, tumbling stream. That same vibrant current flows in you, too. It might be a different hue, but what colour is your love?

* * * * *

* * * * *

I am not just transgender woman; that is not my real identity. Is being a woman your only identity? That comes last. You are an artist; you're a fashion designer, (you could be anyone talented) etc.

I am an actor. I act in theatre as well as in films. I am an artist. I do paintings, and I sell my paintings and fund the education of underprivileged transgender women. And I write poetry. My journey continues. My gender identity is not all of me... I am a human being. I am an Indian. I am an artist. I am an activist. I am a writer. And my transgender identity, or transsexual, or hijra, whatever they call me, is the least I am bothered about.

Harvard Speech, February 2017

* * * *

* * * * *

We don't wait for an invitation to celebrate ourselves. But when we do, we do it fully—dressing up, cooking, dancing and laughing. And we talk. We talk about how women, cis or trans, are still objectified, still silenced, still fighting to be seen as more than just bodies.

* * * * *

* * * * *

Reservation in jobs and education is a right of the marginalized transgender persons and we have been denied that systematically. We still don't have reservations in jobs or education. We still struggle for healthcare, and human dignity. There's so much work left to do.

* * * * *

* * * * *

The transgender community faces severe discrimination, denied jobs and forced into sex work and begging. This systemic exclusion leads to a cycle of poverty and marginalization. It must change, we will fight it to change.

* * * * *

* * * * *

Some trans women don't care about passing. They own their bodies, their voices, their identities. That is real fashion, real power.

* * * * *

* * * * *

I never set out to be a role model. I just wanted to fight. And my fight became my life.

* * * * *

* * * * *

Frida Kahlo taught me that even with pain, you can create something extraordinary. And that is what I try to do.

* * * * *

* * * * *

I imagine myself in their position. I don't just watch and write. I live their pain and my pain, I breathe it, and that's how poetry flows.

* * * * *

* * * * *

People think womanhood is about how you look, how you speak, how you carry yourself. But for me, being a woman is about fighting for dignity—mine and others.

* * * * *

* * * * *

Life for us may be black and white inside, full of struggles. But outside, we make it colourful—with our saris, our makeup, our art and our resistance.

* * * * *

* * * * *

I don't stay with the pain. I rise with it. I break it, I challenge it, I transform it.

* * * * *

* * * * *

We want empathy,
we want inclusion,
we want opportunities,
we want dignity,
we want respect.

* * * * *

* * * * *

In today's world, a cis woman or a trans woman has to be content with her body, with herself, with her inner peace, and accepting of herself. If you are one, understand that the most important thing, regardless of where you were born, how you are, and all else, what truly gives one strength—whether you're male, female, transgender, intersex, or whatever—is accepting yourself exactly as you are.

* * * * *

Musings

From the Diaries

Back in October 2007:

Whatever your face becomes, whatever your body becomes, whatever your cheeks, your hair, your stomach, your hands become, the only important thing is what your thoughts become. How your attitude is, what you say? What you do? How do you perceive the world. That is the important thing in the world of human relationships.

And then in July 2023:

Your body will age but never let your mind age, be alive and keep learning. Never feel older, withered, used and never give up. Age is just a number; time is a myth. Ride the chariots of time in majestic grace. Read, Shine, Connect with the universe.

* * * * *

Back in August 2007:

What is being a woman? The Grace, the beauty, the gestures, the body or the style? Not that. The woman is not that. These are projections of being a woman.

External elements that do not inspire, influence and bring long time change in life.

Being a woman is a deep experience. It is about understanding and accepting oneself as you are. It is about loving oneself and the same way loving others. It is about caring for the suffering beings. It is about identifying the struggling human beings and caring for them. It is about being more than a man. It is about being courageous, skilful, continuously learning, being bold, pursuing knowledge and fighting against miseries.

Being a woman is a lot (of) passionate work, passionate about life, passionate about people, passionate about change, about knowledge and finding God in oneself and others That brings the real woman in you. That is the real woman. It is not about fighting for your rights but showing and proving that you are worth it.

You are precious. You are exceptional. You are divine. Extraordinary people have always suffered in this world. That is their blessing (and the curse). Transgender women are God's children. Celestial beings on Earth. Our lives touch the extremes We are extremely happy and extremely sad.

Being a woman is not about being in disguise. It is about opening your heart, give away all your love and care for the people. You will then discover the true power of being a woman. The femininity will come to you. Your womanhood will blossom herself. You don't need to pursue her. She grows in you. She does not stand alone; she is not misfit in the society. She is an important person (and) the one who changes destiny.

And then in February 2025:

Did I write that? Argh...!

Being a woman is taking charge of your life, being healthy, pursuing your dreams, running after your passions, economically and socially self-dependent without guilt and living free.

* * * *

Then in September 2007:

I love to dance in the rain and also probably get to the soil and roll and get dirty and mud. Only mud all over the face and body. Me alone, or with friends with kids, with family dancing in the rain is one of the happiest and gifted times of my life.

I remember that day when I and Santosh were (playing in the rain) near that grassland at Krishna Dam We were chasing each other and he was chasing me, and I was chasing him. And we were so happy then Id like to live all those moments with him again. Okay, I must plan about my home trip now Keep things and build a list of things to be taken home and keep them My new phone is not so attractive, but I like it. People have all these 7000 ten thousand, twelve thousand, 15,000 17,000 cell phones And I wonder why people need such costlier phones This guy, Magesh Babu of Telugu movies, is cool, right? I like him. And yesterday, I watched a lot of videos and I liked Kate Winslet also. Some horror stuffs were really horrified Oh my god, scary!

I don't want to fall back to my old, horrible depression days when I was thinking always about that idiot. Okay, now the age factor I have seen people get shocked, amused, surprised, and get a little suspicious about my age. Well..well... I am ageless, and I can only say that, live that, feel that I don't know how to live according to my age and I don't care I live my life as I need.

And then in February 2025:

I still love to dance in the rain, I still love Santhosh, I still like Mahesh babu and Kate Winslet and I am aging gracefully and shamelessly.

* * * * *

Essays

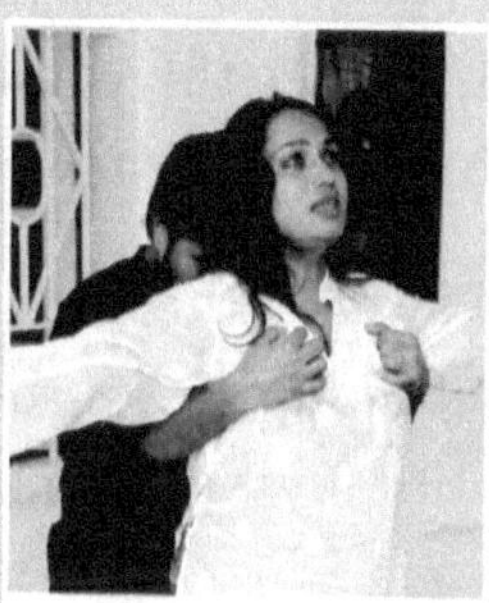

ACTIVISM

FIGHTING FOR EQUALITY AND INCLUSION

Why I Chose to Be an Activist?

I remember that day very clearly. Of what happened to Manju. But before that I must start from here....

I was 12-13 years old and was constantly bullied at school every day for being 'the boy who is feminine". Fearing and hating school, classes and teachers, I used to regularly escape classes the whole day and hide in parks and nearby forests of my town Pollachi.

I sat all day alone, idly looking at the trees, birds and the caged animals in the park. In the caged animals, I could see and identity myself so much. I felt that they were trapped like me too. Only that, I was moving freely but trapped inside. My emotions were trapped, my gender expressions were questioned, I was laughed at, all because I was born a boy, but was feminine. I was a complete woman inside ready to explode and express, it is how it felt then.

On some evenings, I met people like me who were also known then as *Aravanis*, the transgender ladies. I instantly connected with them. We soon became friends. We met secretly in our transgender friends' homes, would lock it (so neighbours wouldn't see) and put on make-up and costumes and wow.. we were ourselves, beautifying our real authentic selves and dancing, cooking, singing, making jokes, laughing out loud. Those were real moments of magic.

Once out of the secret happy rooms and entering into the world, it was so tragic and traumatic for me to see how my friends were treated by their own families. My transgender mentor Apsara amma's brother tried to throw kerosene on her and burn her because he felt so shameful that his 'brother is a transgender person'.

The other friend of mine Saroja (name changed) ran away to Delhi and became a sex worker. In a few years she also became HIV positive. She was not even informed about her mother's death. She still lives in Pune, she has built her own house now after so many years and earns by dancing and blessing. She regularly sends money to her elder sister who lives 10 miles from my home. In the last 20 years, I saw her only twice.

And then the day Manju was raped. I remember that day very clearly. Manju (name changed) was an abandoned transgender girl, driven away by her family. To support her livelihood, she did sex work. She was kidnapped and raped by seven men one night. She never went to the police. "They will point at me that I am a prostitute and this will happen to me". Manju died in AIDS an year later.

The tears, trauma, anger, blood, wounds, fear and pain engulfed in my teenage years, of which I was a witness and a victim, is what made me an activist for the transgender persons of India. The family rejection is the root cause of all our miseries. Left on the streets and driven away, we were and are easily exploited by anyone from the society. When our community steps out of their parental homes, they are also stepping out of their education, bright future, dignity, security, safety and protection.

We in India are preparing to celebrate our 75th Indian Independence. But the transgender and the LGBQIA+ community is being continuously systematically ignored and (or) discriminated, the transgender and gender non-conforming children still go through so much of bullying and violence at schools. My heart breaks when even after all these years, I still continue to read news where a student from Faridabad was bullied for his sexuality and committed suicide.

In the last 18 years, I have lost more than 10 of my transgender friends to suicide, murder and alcohol. In 2011, I wrote the article Dying Young – The death of two young transsexual women in my blog. Little has changed so far when it comes to family inclusion, protection of gender non-conforming children against bullies at schools, sensitizing the academicians to be sensitive and sensible in protecting the students.

This is exactly the reason why I continue to speak, write, paint, perform about the uncared, abandoned lives of thousands of transgender persons in our country who need to be embraced and included in the mainstream society.

Activists like me still face so many challenges to empowering transgender community's lives. Here are some challenges:

- Religious, cultural, superstitious beliefs jeopardies our relationships with our biological families and puts a guillotine in the betterment of our future
- Lack of basic education prevents them from accessing satisfyingly paying jobs
- Discrimination and family rejection drives them to depression and suicide
- Systematic discrimination in the legal, medical and academic fields prevents the community from freely and fearlessly approaching them for their needs.
- Lack of sensitive and inclusive LGBTQI+ workplace policies leave our community to be vulnerable to rejection and discrimination.

How can you make a change?

- First educate yourself about gender identities and sexual orientations.

- Know why it is okay to be a gay, lesbian, bisexual, transgender or intersex.
- I am not sure if you can teach your parents but you sure can teach your own family and siblings. Do you feel that it is a taboo topic to discuss at home? Not anymore!
- Be an ally in supporting human rights of the LGBTQIA+ community.
- Stand up, Voice Out and Loud when a transgender is shamed in public.
- One's gender identity or sexual orientation is just one part of who they are, there may be so many talents and contributions from them which they can offer to the world only when they feel inclusive and appreciated.
- Is your college/university inclusive and have a club or a council for LGBTQI+ students to approach in case if they harassment issues? If not, start a petition to do so.
- Is your company / corporate inclusive and giving employment opportunities for LGBTQI+ persons? Do they practice DEIB? Does your company have an inclusive workplace policy for the community? If not, take action to start initiating it.
- When media is mindless, insensitive, homophobic or transphobic, revolt against such misleading portrayals by writing to them or

writing to the newspapers whoever they are. Or just make a good film that tells the truth :).

- Finally, remember the slogan - My body, my rights. It is for you and me and for everyone of course.
- The future is for diverse people, the future is for non-binary, the future belongs to everyone. Those organizations, corporates, governments and societies which are inclusive, the future will be shaped by them. That is my work prediction.

* * * * *

Fight for Women's
rights cannot be
separated from the
fight for
Transgender rights
as equality for one is
equality for all.

My Frida

My Frida

If there is one artist who had a great influence in my life, my art and fashion, it is Frida Kahlo. Not only am I inspired by her style of art alone, but also by her as a person, all of her. Frida was so many, she was an artist like me, a queer woman, a disabled person, a heart broken human who could never become a biological mother to a child, much like a transgender woman, she was absolutely raw and creative.

Frida's portrait is the most painted portrait in my art life. In a span of a decade, I have created so many portraits of Frida and they are in the walls of homes, museums and office's all over the world. Every time I look into the painting of Frida Kahlo, the ones she created, my heart melts, and I can only feel empathy, compassion and admiration for her. How beautifully and courageously she portrayed her tragic life. Transferring her pain in to art was a genius process. I am not only astonished, but also wonder her truthfulness and talent.

She should have never fallen in love with Diego Rivera, but then love is blind, isn't it? It was fate that united them and it was the same fate that separated and reunited them again. In so many ways her life has mirrored mine, no. I must rephrase that sentence. My life has mirrored hers.

Art makes me forget time and space. Every moment of art that I make, every minute, every hour is my meditation. It is my biggest refuge, and makes me forget my past, not brood about the future and be present in the moment fully in which I consciously exist. It is art that kept me alive during the entire years of pandemic. It kept me mindful, occupied, sane, balanced, creative and fulfilled my financial needs during such difficult times.

Art pushes me to experiment constantly, in my books 'Kuri Aruthean' (குறி அறுத்தேன்), 'We Are Not The Others', and 'Oru Thirunangaiyin Diary Kurippu (ஒரு திருநங்கையின் டைரிக் குறிப்பு), I created all the illustrations for every piece of my poem and writing. Art deceives my time and I hope to live through my painting as much Frida does.

Frida created her own iconic fashion. The beautiful skirts she flaunted, the flower crowns that flawlessly fit and trumpeted her beauty, the jewellery that lay proudly on her are her signature looks. She continues to inspire millions of women, queer and trans persons around the world. In my fashion label, I have created sarees that are digital prints of my paintings of Frida and have worn it in landmark events in my life. When I drape my Frida art saree, like a child being embraced by her mother, I feel safe and content. I launched my fashion label Kals with a photoshoot in Times Square, New York wearing the very first Frida saree I created. I keep paying tribute to the legend whenever and wherever I can. While I am writing this, there is an unfinished portrait of Frida that I haven't completed in two years. There is something beautiful about an unfinished work of art. Is it really unfinished? Should I leave her at that because she is still beautiful. It is time to birth her.

Frida is Forever, I celebrate her now and always will.

* * * * *

Kals

Dress Your Authenticity

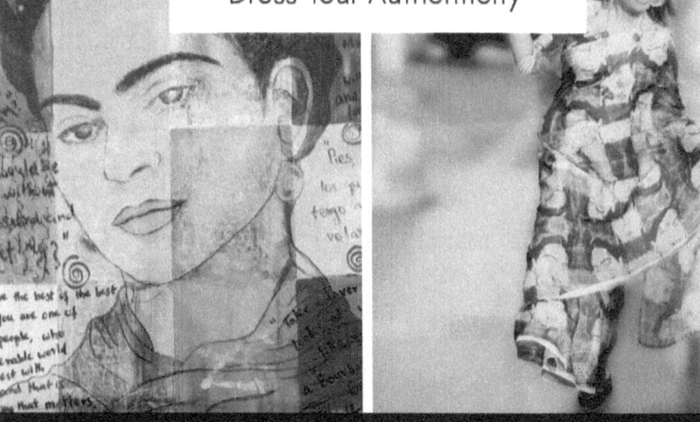

Fashion isn't a Statement, it is Empowerment

In 2019, I organized the first LGBTQI Pride Walk in Coimbatore, But the very first official Pride Walk I organized was in 2010, only six people participated and they were all transwomen from Sahodari Foundation. Nine years and a lot has changed, we had made progress for our rights. So, we must unite and celebrate right?

I wore a red georgette multiple layered and frilled gown with full hand red gloves and red ankle boots. On the streets, I walked and danced in the front wearing a Frida Kahlo inspired flower bandana in rainbow colours. I swivelled and tapped on the street much to the wondering eyes of the passersby and the police who came for the protection. I danced all along the two kilometres non-stop. By the time I finished, my shoes were broken, my red gown's edges were spoilt and I was in complete sweat. But I was in euphoria, so happy and delighted that I wore what I wanted to, a dress 'supposedly' not meant for the street, I broke it. I wore a dress that brought happiness to me. That is how most transgender and gender non-conforming people are! We dress for ourselves and not to impress the world.

During my struggling teenage years as a gender confused kid, I was fascinated by Sridevi's shiny red gold gown she wore in 'Hawa Hawaii' song in the film '*Mr. India*' indeed I found an old saree of my mother, cut it, sewed my own similar '*Mr. India*' dress. What a delight I had when I wore it... I even made a crown and put it on my head. I felt like Miss India.

The yellow saree with a sleeveless blouse Sridevi wore in Chandni, the ribbons, bangs and the velvet overalls in '*Chalbaaz*', they all inspired me to save money and do a rampage of shopping. I have shamelessly copied Sridevi multiple times, no shame at all since I adore her that much. Whenever I used to secretly meet my transgender friends, we all had our own role models, favourite stars and exhibited ourselves so colourfully and danced in our secret dress parties. We all wore only what we loved. Who cares fashion, it was all about wearing and expressing yourself in whatever makes you happy.

In the transgender communities, there are multiple stereotypes about expressing your femininity, for example you need to have long hair and know how to do hairdos and should know how to wrap a saree gracefully. If you don't know then you are not a 'complete woman' or a 'perfect transwoman'. I don't believe these things makes us 'perfect woman'.

As a teenager, I never really liked to wear a saree, but I do wear it now because it brings the graceful and the ultimate femininity in me. My friends say I look gorgeous in a saree than any other dress. Personally, I prefer to dress in a long chiffon or georgette gown which I longed as a child, an unfulfilled childhood fantasy, a child's secret need at that time. I wanted to be that girl with a flower and fruits crown, I wanted to be like snow white but wanted to dress better than her.

I always wanted to be a fairy tale princess, may be because as a teenager, I could never completely express the little girl in me. All I could do was, secretly imagine and draw myself in scraps of paper as a girl in flowing gowns and later hide them or throw them in the dustbin before anyone can see. Those drawing were so healing. Later in life, that is how art became my medium of expression. I took up painting too.

The internet was booming but it was more used by us trans people to find information on medical transition, hormone therapy, sex realignment surgery but not for purchasing a dress. Online shopping hadn't yet arrived in the 90s.

With in the transwomen's circles, we all do research on the 'perfect female look'. If one person in the gang is finding the secrets of perfect flawless skin or a makeup secret, the others will find the best kept secrets for hairless hands and legs, best shops for perfect cholis, sarees, padded push bras, wigs, bangles and anklets. We had all the information about the best products at the cheapest prices available in the markets.

Since I was one of the few who could speak and read English, our friends will collect magazines like Elle, Vogue, Vanity fair and Femina from the old book markets and we sit together and marvel at the dresses the models wore. We used to crack jokes on the models who were deadly thin. More than the magazines, it was always our mothers, sisters and Indian film stars who inspired us with their new collection of jewellery and sarees.

Every year during the summer, the Koothandavar transgender festival happens at Kuvagam village near Villupuram town in Tamil Nadu, India. During my struggling days in male identity, this place was my haven and heaven. This is the hub for all the transgender community who openly were living with their authentic identities. For those who have been living secretly and use this festival to express our true and authentic selves, clothing was the ultimate way to express your personality. Every one of us wanted to be the best, bold, beautiful and gorgeous girl.

The festival's three days will be busting with all sorts of transgender people with fashionable jewels and clothing walking on the roads, there will be beauty pageants and fashion ramp walks as well. All we needed was an accepted space to express our true identities and here it was, the festival which made us all so happy and brought the very exotic and beautiful side of us.

We used to prepare for the festival at least 40 days before. Discussions on shopping for sarees, jewellery, make up, footwear, wigs and accessories will go on and on. Every purchase was dreamy and full of fun. The choice of dresses was all about what we liked, not about what was in vogue or the current trends. We wore our personalities.

Kuvagam was a celebration diverse humans coming out and being themselves, their uniqueness and spectrum of spectacular expressions and gender identities. Those days before the transition, transgender people who live in closets wait all through the year for those three days. Those three days in Villupuram Town and Kuvagam Village are unforgettable.

They are days when all gorgeousness is unleashed and found on all streets shining in all colours walking without fear, without shame and hearts full of happiness and excitement. The festival was the place, a place which became the ground for all activism and visibility in 90s and 2000s uniting voices of people who need to be heard.

The colourful festival brought visibility about the rights of the transgender people in India, being one of the prime reasons for today's milestone victories in transgender rights in India. Yes, our fashion was an undisputed way of Expressing who we are and what we deserve and our own space in the civil society.

Fashion is transformational. Fashion ignites revolution.

Today, as an artist and designer, I explore, experiment and create fashion by transforming my art in to fashionable garments. My start up Kals Apparel (www.kals.in) is a unique initiative where I and my team of transgender artists and designers create awesome outfits that are unique, gorgeous, sustainable and beautiful. I hope this dream will be a reality and will support more and more transgender persons livelihood and transform their lives better.

* * * * *

Fashion is flaunting
your persona
unapologetically and
baring your true self
with Pride.

On A Mission to Empower India's Transgender Community, One Painted Palm at a Time

I remember my childhood so vividly. Until the age of 11, I was a playful, happy child at home, and a good student at school.

Growing up in rural India, I was considered the more privileged child among my two sisters, having been born male. Yet, deep inside, I longed to be my true self.

I was a naturally effeminate child. I felt uncomfortable being addressed as "he," and it seemed like there was this girl inside who liked everything a little girl of my age liked. This made me a constant target. But I didn't fear those big, bullying boys and would fight back, never ashamed of who I was.

Then, at the age of 14, I gave up. After I started losing interest in school, certain teachers became aggressive and would punish me with a cane. I could never tell my parents. Amid painful episodes of shame and self-doubt, I considered ending my own life, though my family's love stopped me from doing so. I avoided attending classes and would go to parks and forests to get away from everyone. Under the trees, I wrote poetry and imagined my future life in drawings, which helped me heal my inner wounds.

When I finally came out as a transgender person to my parents, I was taken to a psychiatrist to help with my gender dysphoria (the distress caused by the discrepancy between a person's body and their gender identity). He asked me to draw how I saw myself in the future, so I drew a beautiful girl with a long skirt, hat and a big smile. He was taken aback, but he eventually helped me gain my family's acceptance.

This is the dilemma faced by teen children with gender dysphoria. Unable to bear the bullying but terrified of disappointing their parents, they fear going to school and they fear dropping out, too. If they "out" themselves, only a few are accepted by their parents.

The deepest wounds cannot heal until they are expressed. Practicing art helps us heal emotional injuries, by providing a safe opportunity for self-expression and shaping one's identity. When our families reject us, we find solace and refuge with other "hijras" or "Thirunangais" who are also struggling to survive. In my lifetime, I have lost many transgender friends to suicide. Other friends died from AIDS.

As a teenager, I witnessed – and was the victim of harassment. A transgender friend of mine, who was a sex worker, was raped by seven men. Another friend was chased by her own brother wanting to burn her. While another friend was driven out by her family. These childhood experiences built my raging desire for justice and inspired me to become an activist for the transgender community.

After completing my master's degree in journalism, I started a magazine called Sahodari (or "sister") to reach out to and support the transgender community. I used photographs, art and text to educate people about mental health, transitioning and their right to dignity. Within a few years, I had founded the Sahodari Foundation and trained our team in visual storytelling.

Art has helped me identify my self-worth. It has been a medium for me to express my hope, joy, fear, anguish, desires and struggles. It is a reflection of my deep self that mirrors my journeys. It is a divine experience. When I paint, it is like my blood flows into the canvas and there is a soul connection. My artworks "The Purple Princess" and "I with in" celebrate the pure feminine and androgynous expressions with bright fluorescent colours. More recently, I have started to incorporate augmented reality and Artificial Intelligence into my artworks – technologies that will help provide another level of meaning and emotional engagement with audiences.

Many people in the community are artistic and creative, but they seldom have the opportunity to practice their art. I realized that our community could not only express themselves through art, they could make a living from it. That is how our *Thoorikai* project was born. I travelled with my team to several cities and small towns in south India to offer free workshops on expressive painting. It has been a therapeutic experience for the participants. When they are making art, they forget time.

We have exhibited the community's artworks in galleries, universities, colleges and public spaces. The reception had been tremendously positive. When people see the artwork, they can identify and empathize with us.

Each piece of art tells a story. Abinaya's "The Struggling Sex Worker" was a moving work, very raw in portraying the exploitation of trans bodies. Viji D's "Begging Cycle" expresses the anguish of asking for money from strangers in trains to meet her basic needs. Nayanthara's "Finding Oneself" is beautiful, spiritual and powerful.

The deepest wounds cannot heal until they are expressed. Practicing art helps us heal emotional injuries, by providing a safe opportunity for self-expression and shaping one's identity. It can bring out our beautiful side. It can make us more tolerant of differences – and of one another.

Sexual violence is a terrible, horrible, health-affecting issue that transgender people have endured for decades. Research from the Indian states of Maharashtra, Tamil Nadu and Karnataka found that four in 10 transgender people will experience some form of sexual abuse before the age of 18. Many of us remain silent victims. But in the Red Wall project testimonials, I understood that all transgender persons have been sexually abused.

The Red Wall Project was created to empower the voices of India's transgender and gender-diverse people, and to help resist the crimes perpetrated against us. It is a community "artivism" project whereby participants are interviewed by my team and write down their experiences of assault, abuse or rape on paper marked with their palm prints in red paint.

Listening to the experiences can be traumatizing, yet we are determined to do it. If we don't tell our community's stories, who will?

With their consent, we bring these stories to the public. During the exhibitions, I use my poetry and performance art to provoke dialogue about taking action against gender-based crimes. We want to reach out to India's young people with our stories, and tell them that it is unacceptable to hurt people based on their gender identity. Through victims' first-hand accounts, we can show them that we are human beings who deserve better treatment, respect and dignity.

Whenever we exhibit these testimonials, I see people reading them patiently for hours. I have seen visitors who, after reading, sit in silence in tears. Young people come to me and say, "What can I do to stop this violence? How can I be supportive?" And I tell them: "Educate yourself more, sensitize your family and your friends to be trans-friendly. Empathize with us. That is all we need."

For decades, our community has struggled for acceptance and equality. In 2014, hard-fought battles led to a milestone victory when India's Supreme Court finally recognized transgender people as a "third gender." It was a move I had long lobbied the judiciary for, and the legal recognition meant, for instance, that people could enrol at academic institutions, as openly transgender, without fear.

Many corporations have started to hire transgender employees. Years of activism and awareness-building have resulted in many other welcome changes, including the positive portrayals of transgender people in mainstream media and films. In January 2020, the Transgender Persons (Protection of Rights) Act came into effect, providing further legal protections of our rights and welfare.

There is still much work to be done. We are still fighting for affirmative action to ensure jobs and places at educational institutions. We want protection against stigma and discrimination, and legal guarantees that the punishments for crimes against transgender people will be severe.

But the rainbow is shining bright and beautiful. I see hope. I see a better future for our generation of queer Indians. I see India as a place that can uphold LGBTQI rights in the world. And I see India as a pioneer of transgender rights in the future.

* * * * *

No one has the authority to determine, judge, deny, decide or label my body, and my gender. It is My Body, My Rights, My Rules.

Third Gender Recognition: Tamil Transgender Women in the Forefront and Our Pioneering Work

It was August 14th, 2010.

The day before the 63rd Independence Day of India. The golden day when the first seed for legal recognition of India's third gender people was sown. The venue was Madras Judicial Academy.

It was an important day when some of the highest Judicial Authorities gathered in the Chennai, the capital of Tamil Nadu state. Department of Social Welfare of the Tamil Nadu government, Madras High Court, Tamil Nadu State Legal Services Authority, National Legal Services Authority and the Madras Judicial Academy joined hands and organized the event 'Seminar on issues related to the transgender community'. This was the first event when the highest judiciary of India could hear the transgender community's dilemma in person, face to face, heart-to-heart. This was the event that tore open for the truths to bear all, the event that sensitized some of the country's greatest change makers.

Chief Justice of the Indian Supreme Court Altamas Kabir, Chief Justice of the Madras High court M.Y. Iqbal, Supreme court Judge Shri Sadasivam, Minister of Social Welfare Geetha Jeevan, Director of the Department of Social Welfare Mrs. Nirmala and the state one of the highest Police official Archana Ramachandran were the prominent participating guests in the event.

Once the protocol speeches were over, it was time for us, the transgender community to speak. I, as a representative of the community, I had been waiting for this great opportunity to present the problems faced by our transgender people. I was on the dais sitting opposite the Honourable Chief Justice of the Supreme Court Altamas Kabir giving him an emotional speech supported by a PowerPoint presentation on the problems faced by the transgender people of India. Furthermore, I started from childhood, teenage and went to speak to the Judge about what dilemma and terror we faced in schools as transgender kids, the bullying, the harassment, the lack of understanding and counselling support, the life in fear and depression at such a young age. I spoke to the Judges in detail about the discriminations faced by us in the public, the lack of education that has ultimately resulted in the community to resort to begging and sex work. Abandoned by family and becoming beggars and sex workers, all our dreams crashed, we become unwanted people in the society. He was moved and became very emotional. Bringing that compassion and his understanding was a success, I was so happy to see that he was fully committed and listening to my every word.

After my presentation speech, activist Priyababu spoke in detail about the possible solutions for the problems faced by the community, senior activist Noori and community voices Noorjahan and Selvi Santhosh also spoke about the problems transgender women face in the society.

This was the first event in the Indian history when the transgender community could directly speak in detail about our problems to the country's Supreme court Judges who were the members of National Legal Services Authority (NALSA).

After this event, on 4th February 2011 National Legal Services Authority with technical support from United Nations Development Program organized a National Seminar at Vigyan Bhavan in New Delhi. The Seminar was titled 'Transgender and the Law'. This was the first National seminar that discussed the legal rights and recognizing the third gender people of India.

The man who was responsible for initiating this seminar was the then Supreme court Judge and the head of NALSA, Honourable Shri. Altamas Kabir sir.

This seminar was the follow-up of the first seminar held in Chennai.

Hundreds of Judges from all over India, including some of the prominent supreme court, high court and district court Judges were present in the event. The highest-ranking Police officers from all over the country were also present in the event. It was a historical day in the transgender rights movement. Along with Honourable Justice Altamas Kabir sir who was also the Executive Chairman of NALSA, were other eminent Judges like the Chief Justice of the Madras High Court M.Y. Iqbal, New Delhi High Court Chief Justice Deepak Mishra and Justice Vikramajit Sen. UNDP Country Director Caitley Weisen was present at the event as well.

As activists and transgender community representatives, I and Priyababu were the two people from the South of India who were there to do presentations and deliver speeches to sensitize the officials. From the North of Indian were Gauri Sawant, Laxmi Narayan Tripathi and Sabeena Francis.

The highlight of this seminar was the speeches and presentations by the transgender activists which aimed to sensitize the Judiciary on the problems of the transgender people of India whose life can only see ray of hope and an equal life like any other citizen of the country. After the protocol speeches by the chief guests and the hosts of the event, the Judges and Police officers were requested to be seated in two different halls. It was time for us to speak. I and Priyababu were in a hall and Lakshmi Narayan Tripathi, Gauri Sawant and Sabeena were in the other speaking, answering and interacting with the Judges on the transgender people's lives in India. I was sitting next to Chief Justice sir, a very noble and kind person. He was listening to me very carefully and during his speech I could see how much of a deep understanding he has on transgender issues.

Lawyer Laya Medhini from Article 39, Dr. Venkatesh Chakrapani, Akila Das from CFAR, Ernest Noronha from UNDP and Sonal Mehta were some of the people who were present there. Ernest Noronha's amazing background work on the transgender rights issue is notable here. Working in UNDP, transgender rights have been one of the key issues close to his heart, and he has contributed tremendously for the community's legalization and empowerment in a big way through UNDP.

Following this seminar, a number of meetings and seminars were organized by State Legal Services Authorities of various states. I spoke at the Maharashtra State Legal Services Authority's seminar and at the seminar organized by Guwahati University in Assam. I was invited by the National Judicial Academy and once again and met Judiciary from all over the country and lectured them insisting the very importance of legalizing our gender and procuring our rights. Furthermore, I also spoke at the Jindal Global School of Law on the same issue stressing on acknowledging our rights as citizens of this country.

Activist Jeeva Rangaraj spoke at the State Judicial meeting at Raichur and at Hyderabad, Olga and Bharati Kannamma also spoke at various meetings. At the district level Judicial meetings, Sangeetha spoke at Coimbatore, Kajol at Trichy and Viji at Tuticorin did their best to take the issue in front of the Judiciary and voiced for social justice and legal recognition for transgender people.

Akkai did the work in Karnataka following in the steps of her predecessors like Pamela and Revathi, Seetha and Rudhra Chetri did it at New Delhi, Ranjita Sinha and Amrita Sarkar did fabulous work in West Bengal. There were a number of activists from other states who did similar work with passion for determination for our rights and recognition.

The result of the great hard work by transgender women in sensitizing the Judiciary of India and advocating for our rights finally reaped its results. NALSA filed a Social Justice Litigation with the Supreme Court of India in 2013. The case was known as NALSA v/s Union of India. After almost a year and a half, on 15th April 2014 the Supreme Court of India recognized transgender people legally. It also directed the state and central government to take proactive measures.

For almost a decade, UNDP has done tremendous groundwork and has supported in our battle towards legal recognition of the third gender.

There are countless legal forums and seminars I had participated and voiced for our rights. With no money or power, individual transgender persons have done so much for the rights and respect of our vulnerable community in our country. From filing a public interest litigation for basic human rights, baring all our lives and our pains courageously in public hearings, to protesting fearlessly for every right of ours on the streets, it is an indisputable fact that the Indian transgender movement's battle for legal recognition started in Tamil Nadu. I say it with great pride that the Tamil trans women have contributed largely and powerfully by voicing for the community's rights and taking actions in the right direction in our country. Certainly, the legal recognition of third gender would not have been possible without the immense contribution of Trans women from Tamil Nadu.

April 15th, the day the transgender people were recognized legally in India, should be announced by the government of India as the National Transgender Day.

A historic day indeed! So proud that our years of hard work have finally brought recognition to our community. We Made It! Yet, we have a long way to go, we are not tired and we are not giving up and we will make sure history not be forgotten.

* * * *

Climate Change is the biggest threat to Transgender persons Future

The transgender community's fight is not only about our human rights and economic safety, it is also about our future - living in a world that guarantees good water, energy, good health and safe housing. Climate change is the biggest threat to the well-being and safety of the transgender community of India.

For example, during the 2004 Tsunami and the Chennai heavy rains in the years 2005, 2015, 2021 and 2024, hundreds of transgender persons were displaced, and many of them lost their homes and remained homeless resulting to many resorting to begging and sex work. The governments do not have any data on how many transgender lives were lost and how many became homeless.

Karthika, a transgender woman running a small idly shop, was one of many whose livelihoods were swept away by the devastating Chennai floods. The loss of her shop left her without any income, forcing her into a precarious struggle for survival, relying on begging and performing blessings. Transgender individuals in Chennai, often residing in flood-prone, low-lying areas, are particularly vulnerable. When disasters strike, their homes and businesses are frequently destroyed, eliminating their means of support. This vulnerability is compounded by existing discrimination and marginalization. Following the floods, many in the transgender community faced immense hardship, relying on charity for basic necessities like food and shelter, with some finding temporary refuge in shelters while others were left to fend for themselves. The disaster had a profoundly damaging effect, leaving many transgender people in Chennai grappling to rebuild their lives.

The vulnerable and marginalised transgender persons do not know their rights and opportunities in spite of the tremendous growth in communication and the internet technologies. Organisations working for the transgender community should focus on sensitizing the vulnerable transgender people on their rights. It is very important to make them understand about the Transgender Protection Act 2019 and the Equal Opportunities Policy introduced by the Ministry of Social Justice and Empowerment. Governments should help the affected persons rebuild with job training and financial support. Stronger social programs are also important. Including transgender people in green jobs initiatives can create long-term opportunities.

Transgender people need to be part of the conversation when governments make climate policies. Our experiences are valuable. Collecting data on how climate change affects our community specifically is important. Public awareness campaigns can help reduce stigma. And budgets should include funding for programs that directly support transgender communities. It's crucial to remember that transgender people face many kinds of discrimination, and climate policies must address all of these. Working together – governments, organizations, and transgender communities – is the only way to make real progress.

"Trans Rights,
Climate Justice!
Our Fight, Our Future!"

The fight for
Transgender rights
is not just about
individual freedoms;
it's about dismantling
a social order
built on exclusion
and oppression.
Reservation is a
crucial weapon
in this struggle
for liberation.

We Bleed on the

"Whoever harms or injures or endangers the life, safety, health or well-being, whether mental or physical, of a transgender person or tends to do acts including causing physical abuse, sexual abuse, verbal and emotional abuse and economic abuse, shall be punishable with imprisonment for a term which shall not be less than six months but which may extend to two years and with fine." says Chapter VIII Section 18 of The Transgender Persons (Protection of Rights) Act 2019.

What justice does this act give to the victims of sexual abuse and rape? The perpetrator is punished with just 6 months to 2 years of imprisonment and fine? Aren't we traumatized as much as when a cis women is raped? Don't we feel the same physical and emotional pain as much like a cis women's body?

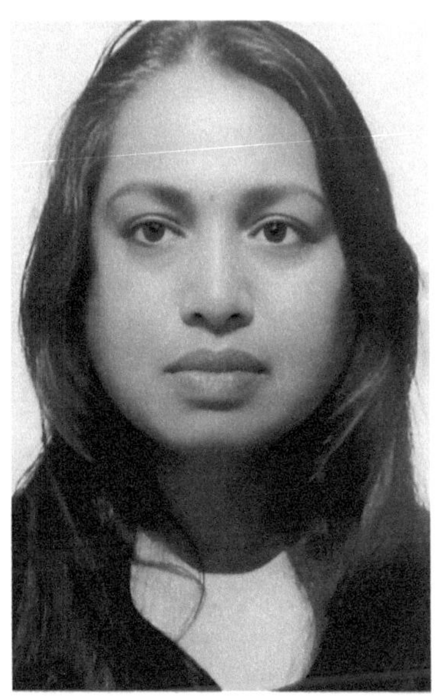

Red Walls

Similar crimes against cis women under laws like Section 376 of the Indian Penal Code (IPC) mandates a minimum of seven years and can extend to life imprisonment or the death penalty for the perpetrator. Why is the punishment lesser when the perpetrator commits the same crime against trans persons?

Aren't our bodies worth it? Aren't we worth it? Won't our genitals, our wounds, our bodies bleed? Won't we cry the same? Wont our tears be salty enough for you to give justice?

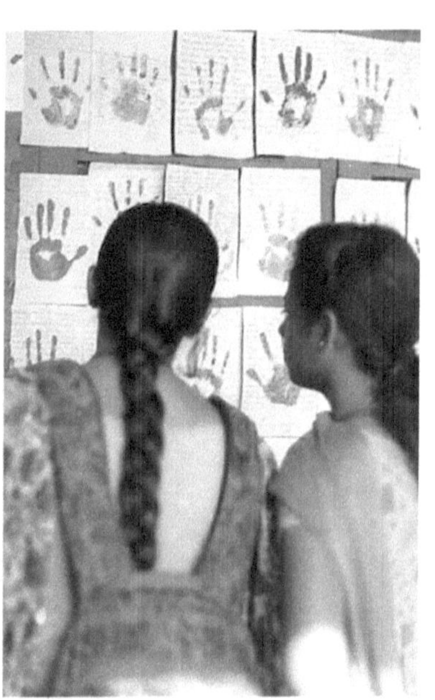

For Justice

Have you ever encountered a news report detailing the conviction of an individual who assaulted a transgender person?

This absence underscores the ineffectiveness of our supposed legal protections. Perpetrators evade punishment, rendering the law impotent.

The mere act of filing a complaint is an enormous struggle. Securing justice through the courts is an intimidating task and as a result many victims remaining silent, and the cycle of violence continues on and on.

For Protection

Society has systematically disregarded our suffering. This is the urgent need for starting the Red Wall Project. I and my team including trans rights activist Sowndharya Gopi from Sahodari Foundation travel through India, documenting the lived experiences of transgender individuals.

Their testimonies, written in their own words and authenticated with their fingerprints, serve as irrefutable evidence of sexual violence they endured.

These documents, bearing the weight of our collective trauma, are presented to the public, exposing the reality of societal injustice.

For Dignity.

We engage with educational institutions, fostering dialogue about the challenges we face and the justice we seek. These testimonies are powerful evidence, similar to sworn confessions.

We are disseminating these documents to judicial bodies and state leaders. We seek protection, justice, recognition and inclusion within society.

WE BELONG!

Stand with us
Voice with us
Fight with us
Against Injustice
Against exploitation
Against violence.

Notes

-184-

Other books by the Author:

குறி அறுத்தேன் – Kuri Aruthean (Tamil)

We Are Not The Others

ஒரு திருநங்கையின் டைரிக் குறிப்பு
(Oru thirunangaiyin Dairy Kurippu – Tamil)

9 798899 618543